101 Spanish Riddles

Understanding Spanish Language and Culture Through Humor

Rafael Falcón

Illustrated by Luc Nisset-Raidon

McGraw-Hill

Chicago New York San Francisco Lisbon London Madrid Mexico City Milan New Delhi San Juan Seoul Singapore Sydney Toronto

Library of Congress Cataloging-in-Publication Data

101 Spanish riddles : understanding Spanish language and culture through humor / Rafael Falcón ; illustrated by Luc Nisset-Raidon.
p. cm.
Includes index.
ISBN 0-658-01505-2
1. Riddles, Spanish. 2. Spanish language—Self-instruction. I. Title: One hundred one Spanish riddles. II. Title: One hundred and one Spanish riddles. III. Falcón, Rafael.

PN6375.A18 2001
468.6'421—dc21 00-51646

McGraw-Hill

A Division of The ***McGraw·Hill*** *Companies*

3 4 5 6 7 8 9 0 LBM/LBM 0 9 8 7 6 5 4 3 2

ISBN 0-658-01505-2

This book was set in ITC American Typewriter.
Printed and bound by Lake Book Manufacturing.

Interior design by Amy Yu Ng

Other titles in this series
101 Spanish Idioms
101 Spanish Proverbs
101 French Idioms
101 French Proverbs
101 Japanese Idioms

This book is printed on acid-free paper.

Contents

Foreword

Riddles have been part of Hispanic folklore for centuries. They have been the center of entertainment while picking coffee, shelling beans, or making tortillas, and despite technological advances in today's world, they continue as an essential component of Hispanic humor and folklore. These word games are utilized to trick, amuse, engage, and mislead participants, creating through that effort both puzzlement and laughter. People of all ages and backgrounds are charmed as their wit is tested and challenged with these short puzzles.

Much of the humor and solutions of Spanish riddles are rendered from the language itself. Many words have several meanings, providing a linguistic source from which a good and effective riddle can be created. An example is the riddle "¿Por qué el perro le ladra al automóvil?" (*Why does the dog bark at a car?*) The response is "porque el automóvil lleva un gato en el baúl" (*because the car has a "gato" in the trunk*). This answer provides a playful resolution because the word "gato" refers to both a cat and a car jack.

This collection of common Spanish riddles includes a variety of solutions. The answer for some of these puzzles rests upon knowledge of an idiomatic expression. At times, the resolution requires putting several words together within the riddle. In others, the wording is skillfully manipulated so as to mislead the focus of attention. As such, these 101 riddles provide a fun and entertaining way to learn the Spanish language and culture.

101 Spanish Riddles is divided into 10 sections based upon the theme of the riddle or the linguistic style utilized in its presentation. Admittedly, this logical grouping hints at the nature of the puzzles included in that category. An illustration, the Spanish answer, and the English translation of the riddle and answer accompany each riddle. An explanatory note follows those containing more advanced or intricate language usage. In some situations, a dialogue or narrative presents the pivotal vocabulary in contemporary everyday application. Translations of the dialogues or narratives are provided at the back of the book as an extra aid to better understanding the context. An index of the key words in the riddles is also included.

101 Spanish Riddles is an entertaining alternative to help learn language and culture. Whether planning a trip to the Hispanic world, studying Spanish, teaching Spanish as a second language, or simply desiring a taste of Hispanic culture, the reader will want to consult this collection of humorous, poetic, and challenging brainteasers. The wealth of cultural and linguistic information and the testing of cleverness make this book attractive and enjoyable to both native and nonnative speakers of Spanish.

Acknowledgments

I want to express my appreciation to all my Hispanic friends who provided me with riddles. Many of these brainteasers have been passed along from generation to generation, tossed around with passion and laughter, making long trips shorter, enlivening family gatherings, and providing enjoyment for any moment. I especially would like to acknowledge my gratitude to Dennis Díaz, my 10-year-old Costa Rican friend, and doña María Calderón, his 83-year-old grandmother, for renewing for me the fun of riddles in cross-generational action as we traveled many miles in their family van along Costa Rican roads. The collection he prepared for me in his careful penmanship is one of my personal treasures. Tribute also goes to my father, Ramón Falcón, for planting within me an insatiable curiosity to unravel these word puzzles. His favorite, "Alto y alto como un pino y pesa menos que un comino," is included in this compilation.

My gratefulness also extends to my English-language collaborators in this project. I would like to recognize my wife, Christine, for her enthusiastic support for the undertaking, for her many helpful and creative suggestions, and for her work in preparing the manuscript. My colleague and fellow professor Robert Yoder, and friend and librarian Michael Miller, with his love of words and linguistic puzzles, have also provided very important contributions to the quality of this collection.

Finally, I want to verbalize my deep thankfulness for the pleasure of my childhood on the Caribbean island of Puerto Rico, a time rich with games, sports, riddles, and laughter. This has indeed provided a solid base and love for the collection now resting in your hands.

Section One

La gente y la naturaleza

People and Nature

1 Grande muy grande,
arde y no se quema,
quema y no es candela.
¿Qué es?

El sol.

It's large, very large.
It's on fire but is not consumed.
It burns but is not a candle.
What is it?
(The sun.)

A. **El sol** es muy grande y siempre está **ardiendo**. Aunque está lejos de nosotros puede **quemarnos** si nos exponemos demasiado. También sus rayos ultravioletas pueden ser nocivos.
B. Quizás unas cuantas **candelas** no sean tan peligrosas.
A. ¡Pero imagínate cuántas **candelas** necesitaríamos!
B. ¡Muchas, muchas, ciertamente muchísimas!

2 ¿Qué es lo que está al lado tuyo y no lo ves?

Las orejas.

What is beside you but you can't see it?
(Your ears.)

A. ¡Qué **orejas** más grandes tiene Manolín!
B. Sí, tienes razón. Por lo menos él las lleva a todos lados. El problema es que no puede vérselas.
A. Claro, sólo cuando se mira al espejo.

3 ¿Cuál es el árbol que vale más de noche que de día?

Donde duermen las gallinas.

What tree has more value during the night than during the day?
(The tree where the hens sleep.)

In rural areas of Latin America the chickens usually live outdoors, and during the night they gather in a tree in the yard to sleep.

A. Esos árboles de mango no están produciendo. Ya no valen mucho.
B. Por lo menos **las gallinas** duermen ahí de noche.
A. ¡Ja! Esos árboles valen más de noche que de día.

4 Son hermanos muy unidos, dondequiera van juntitos.

Los dedos.

They are brothers, very united.
Everywhere they go, they go together.
(The fingers.)

Los hermanos Marrero son muy **unidos**. Ellos viven en la misma casa, comparten todas sus cosas y siempre viajan juntos. La gente del pueblo dice que ellos son como **los dedos** de la mano que dondequiera van juntitos.

5 Dos cristales transparentes, tienen agua y no son fuentes.

Los ojos.

Two transparent orbs.
They have water
and are not fountains.
(The eyes.)

A. La gente dice que **los ojos** son el espejo del alma.
B. Yo creo que tienen razón.
A. Claro. Son como **dos cristales transparentes** por los que uno puede mirar y ver el interior del ser humano.
B. Oye, Juan, pero qué poético te estás poniendo.

6 Un toro muy negro que sale del mar
ni el perro más bravo lo puede atajar.

La noche.

A very black bull that comes out of the sea
and not even the fiercest dog can stop it.
(The night.)

A. A ese **toro** siempre le gusta salir al campo por **la noche**.
B. Sí, y parece que el reflejo de la luna en el agua lo hace correr con sumo entusiasmo.
A. Sabes, una noche vi al impresionante animal correr tan rápido que ni **el perro** más bravo lo hubiera podido atajar. Parecía que **el toro** se fusionaba con **la noche.**

7 Una señora muy aseñorada que siempre anda mojada. Esta señora rosada está en su cuarto aprisionada.

La lengua.

A very elegant lady
who is always wet.
This pink lady
is imprisoned in her room.
(The tongue.)

A. Marcela, tú hablas de todo el mundo. Parece que siempre estás moviendo **la lengua.**

B. Claro, a esta señora hay que sacarla de su prisión de vez en cuando, ¿verdad?

A. En tu caso, probablemente. Tú dirías que quieres dejarla que se seque. ¡Qué par de mujeres son ustedes!

8 Verde fue mi nacimiento, amarillo fue mi abrir y blanco me voy a quedar para poderte servir.

El algodón.

I was green at birth;
I was yellow at my opening.
Now I will stay white
to be able to serve you.
(Cotton.)

A. A mí me gusta la ropa de **algodón**.

B. ¿Por qué? Hay otros materiales muy buenos.

A. Es que para mí la ropa de **algodón** es fresca, dura mucho y proviene de un proceso natural.

B. Todo esto suena magnífico. ¿Estás segura que esto no es un comercial pagado?

9 Te acompaña donde vas
y está siempre donde estás.
Aunque tú no lo ves,
vivir sin él no podés.

El aire.

It goes with you wherever you go
and is always present wherever you are.
Even though you cannot see it,
you cannot live without it.
(Air.)

A. He leído que hay cuatro elementos que son básicos para la sobrevivencia del ser humano: el agua, la tierra, el fuego y **el aire.**

B. Para mí el más importante e interesante de todos es **el aire.**

A. ¿Por qué **el aire?**

B. Porque, aunque no lo vemos, siempre está con nosotros. Además, no podemos vivir sin él. En otras palabras, **el aire** y yo somos inseparables.

10 Son siete en uno. Coge tus pinceles; no dejes ninguno.

Los colores del arco iris.

They are seven in one.
Grab your paintbrushes;
don't leave out a single one.
(The colors of the rainbow.)

A. Está lloviendo y haciendo sol a la misma vez. Mira, se ha formado un precioso **arco iris.**
B. Apresúrate, busca la cámara y vamos a sacar una foto.
A. Mejor vamos a pintarlo y a acentuar los colores uno a uno.
B. Buena idea, así podemos crear una obra maestra como las de Picasso.
A. ¡Creo que no!

11 Paso por el fuego y no me quemo.
Paso por el río y no me mojo.
Me estiro, me encojo, de goma no soy.
Me marco de noche.
Adivina quién soy.

La sombra.

I go through fire and do not burn.
I pass through the river and I don't get wet.
I stretch and I shrink, but I'm not made of rubber.
I appear at night.
Can you guess who I am?
(A shadow.)

Los dos hombres entraron a la casa abandonada en busca de artefactos valiosos. La oscuridad de la noche no permitió que vieran bien. Repentinamente, ambos vieron algo que parecía estirarse y encogerse mientras ellos se movían. Ambos se quedaron paralizados contenientdo la respiración. Entonces simultáneamente se relajaron, casi riéndose: era sólo su **sombra**.

12 Estaba un mango en el árbol: dos lo vieron, cinco lo agarraron y treinta y dos se lo comieron. ¿Quiénes fueron?

Los dos son los ojos.
Los cinco son los dedos
y los treinta y dos son los dientes.

There was a mango in a tree:
two saw it, five grabbed it, and thirty-two ate it.
Who were they?
(The two are the eyes, the five are the fingers, and the thirty-two are the teeth.)

La viejita, sentada en un banco del parque, cautivaba la atención de los niños con sus adivinanzas. Mientras contaba de los dos, los cinco y los treinta y dos que se habían comido un mango, los oyentes pensaban que ella hablaba de un ejército. "Ah no," se rió entre dientes, "son **los ojos**, **los dedos** y **los dientes** de una sola persona."

Section Two

Los animales y los insectos

Animals and Insects

13 ¿Cuál es el animal que tiene las patitas en la cabeza?

El piojo.

What animal has its little feet on the head?
(A louse.)

A. ¿Cuál es la capital de Argentina?
B. No sé. ¿Santiago?
A. Buenos Aires, Felicia, ¿qué tienes tú en la cabeza?
B. ¿En mi cabeza? Nada, compañero. ¿En mi cabeza? **Piojos**. Montones de **piojos**.

14 ¿Cuál de los animales es aquel cuyo nombre tiene todas las cinco vocales?

El murciélago.

Which animal has all five vowels in its name?
(The bat.)

El esposo apagó la luz y se acostó con su esposa. Como a los dos minutos estaban alarmados por un ruido extraño en la habitación. El hombre, un poco asustado, se levantó y encendió la luz. Para su sorpresa, vieron que era **un murciélago** que ahora colgaba de una cortina. Después de perseguirlo un rato, el animalito salió por la misma ventana por la que había entrado.

15 ¿Cuál es el animal que tiene veinticinco cabezas?

El caballo—veinticuatro cabezas de clavos de las herraduras y la del caballo.

Which animal has twenty-five heads?
(The horse—twenty-four nail heads on the horseshoes and the horse's head.)

El vaquero le llevó **el caballo** al herrero porque **una herradura** estaba floja. El meticuloso artesano amarró al animal por **la cabeza** y procedió a examinar la pata del **caballo.** Descubrió, entonces, que varias **cabezas de clavos** estaban por fuera.

16 ¿Cuál es el animal que después de muerto alborota más?

El chivo—porque usan el cuero para tambor.

Which animal makes more noise after its death than during its life?
(The goat—because its skin is used to make drums.)

En una exploración desconsiderada, el niño se amarró la soga de **un chivo** por el cuello. El quería demostrar que era más fuerte que el animal. **El chivo**, asustado por el halar de la soga, comenzó a correr descontroladamente y arrastró al pequeño explorador por toda la finca. Al irse desenrrollando la soga, el niño quedó con el cuello todo ensangrentado. Se aprendió una lección del incidente: **un chivo** es más fuerte que un niño.

17 ¿Cuál es el animal que cuando cambia de posición cambia el nombre?

El escarabajo.

Which animal changes its name when it changes position?
(The beetle.)

The phrase "es cara abajo," meaning "is face down," sounds like "escarabajo" in normal conversational Spanish. Thus, if the beetle is flipped over, face up, it should be called "es cara arriba."

A. ¿Cuáles son tus pasatiempos?
B. No tengo pasatiempos.
A. Yo colecciono **escarabajos**.
B. Oye, si los pasatiempos ayudan a eliminar el estrés, quizás yo deba comenzar a coleccionar algo.
A. ¿Por qué no coleccionas "es cara arribas"?
B. Tú siempre con tu torcida imaginación.

18 Todos me tienen por buena y yo me tengo por tonta, pues para vestir a otros me quitan a mí la ropa.

La oveja.

Everyone thinks I am good;
I think I am a fool.
To provide apparel for others,
my clothes are taken from me.
(A sheep.)

A. Yo tomo té de manzanilla cuando no puedo dormir.
B. Yo me tomo una taza de leche caliente.
A. Alguna gente cuenta **ovejas**.
B. Yo pienso que eso no funciona. Es sólo un mito.

19 Aunque es corta mi ventura, estreno todos los años un vestido sin costuras de colores salpicado.

La serpiente.

Though my venture is short-lived,
I make a debut each year
in a garment without seams
bespattered all over with colors.
(A snake.)

A. A mí me dan terror **las serpientes**.

B. ¿Por qué? Hay **serpientes** que son inofensivas y no te hacen nada. Otras no te hacen nada a menos que las provoques. **Las serpientes** son importantes en el ciclo de la naturaleza. Además, algunas "se visten" de unos colores bellos.

A. No sé. Es la idea de que pueden estar dondequiera y te pueden picar.

20 Mi madre me hizo una casa sin puertas y sin ventanas, y cuando quise salir, rompí la muralla.

El pollito.

My mother made me a house
without doors and without windows,
and when I tried to get out,
I broke through the wall.
(A chick.)

A. Cuando yo estaba en segundo grado la maestra nos enseñó una canción de **un pollito**.
B. ¡Qué casualidad! La mía también lo hizo en segundo grado.
A. La canción hablaba de **un pollito** que tenía hambre y frío, y decía pío pío. Era una de las canciones más cantadas.
B. Parece que **los pollitos** son mascotas favoritas de los niños.

21 Pasea de noche
y duerme de día.
Le gusta la leche
y la carne fría.

El gato.

It roams about at night
and sleeps during the day.
It likes milk
and cold meat.
(A cat.)

El gato de Federico es grande y negro. Verdaderamente es **un gato** lindo, pero pienso que muy mimado. Pues, el estimado animal sólo sale de noche, bebe sólo leche fresca y demanda que la carne que come tiene que estar en su mejor condición.

22 Por una vocal empieza y por la misma termina. Tiene la vista fina y todo el campo domina.

El águila.

It begins with a vowel
and ends with the same.
Its eyesight is sharp
and it rules the whole field.
(An eagle.)

El águila es un ave impresionante. Cuando vuela parece dominar todo el campo. Hay países que emplean esta ave como símbolo en sus escudos o su sistema monetario. También hay muchos equipos deportivos que utilizan **el águila** como mascota.

Section Three

La comida

Food

23 Tengo cabeza blanca, gruesa cabellera, y conmigo llora toda cocinera.

La cebolla.

I have a white head
and I have coarse hair.
Every single cook
sheds tears with me.
(An onion.)

A. Margarita, pela **las cebollas**, por favor.
B. No, mami, pélalas tú. Estas condenadas siempre me hacen llorar.
A. Mi hija, si no las pelas ahora mismo, yo soy la que te va a hacer llorar.

24 Blanca soy, blanca nací.
Pobres y ricos me comen a mí.
En el agua me hago
y en el agua me deshago.

La sal.

I am white and was born white.
Both rich and poor eat of me.
In water I receive my being
and in water I lose it.
(Salt.)

A. Paco, pásame **la sal**, por favor.
B. Hombre, no debes seguir comiendo tanta **sal**. No es buena para la salud.
A. No será buena para la salud, pero es buena para el paladar.

25 Col parece y flor también. Para adivinarla, únelas bien.

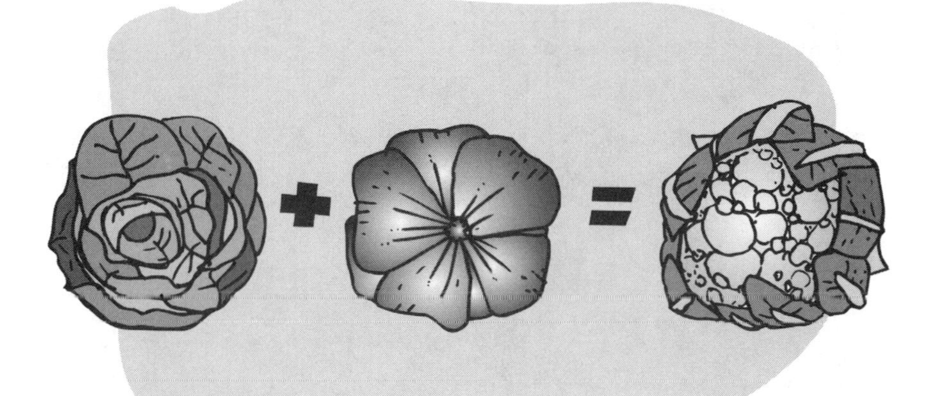

La coliflor.

It looks like a cabbage as well as a flower.
To guess this riddle, put them together.
(Cauliflower.)

A. La gente de hoy día come mucha carne y pocos vegetales.
B. Sí, yo sé: hamburguesas, perros calientes, chuletas.
A. En mi opinión, ¿qué hay mejor que una buena ensalada? Uno le puede poner tomate, lechuga, brócoli y **colifor**. Entonces se le echan varias gotitas de un buen aceitito de oliva, y con una gruesa rebanada de pan casero usted saborea una satisfactoria y saludable comida.

26 Verde me crié, rubio me cortaron, y blanco me amasaron.

El trigo.

I was raised green,
I was harvested golden,
and I was kneaded white.
(Wheat.)

La harina de **trigo** se usa en una infinidad de productos. El sabroso pan en su variedad de formas, las deliciosas galletitas y la gran variedad de repostería, son sólo algunas de las maneras en que se utiliza **el trigo**.

27 Primero fui blanca,
después verde fui.
Cuando fui dorada,
¡ay, pobre de mí!

La naranja.

First I was white,
then I was green.
When I was golden,
ouch, poor me!
(An orange.)

El hombre cruzó la cerca y se subió al árbol en busca de las preciadas y doradas **naranjas**. Él agarró la primera, pero en ese mismo momento oyó la voz de alguien que venía apresuradamente a reclamar sus frutas. El cazador de **naranjas** no quiso esperar a ver la cara del dueño.

28 Tiene corona y no es rey. Se para y no tiene pies. Tiene escamas y no es pescado. Tiene ojos y no ve.

La piña.

It has a crown and is not a king.
It stands upright and has no feet.
It has scales and is not a fish.
It has eyes and does not see.
(A pineapple.)

"Corona" is the stem or top, "escamas" is the peeling, and "ojos" are the dark spots found in the pineapple when it is peeled.

A. ¿Puedes pelar **la piña** para la ensalada de frutas de la cena?
B. Está bien, ¿pero sabes lo que voy a hacer? Voy a guardar **la corona** para plantarla mañana.
A. Buena idea, pero mientras pelas la fruta, asegúrate de sacarle bien **los ojos**.
B. Sí, lo que tú digas. El único problema es que si le saco **los ojos** no va a ver.
A. ¡Qué graciosa! Tú siempre con tus chistes flojos.

29 Tiene dientes y no come. Tiene cabeza y no es hombre.

El ajo.

It has teeth and does not eat.
It has a "cabeza" and is not a man.
(Garlic.)

Besides being the word for teeth, "dientes" is also used in Spanish to depict the cloves in the garlic, while "cabeza" is the term for both a head and the garlic bulb.

Pedro cogió **la cabeza de ajo** y le sacó **un diente**. Luego lo partió en rebanadas y lo hizo un sándwich para ayudarle con el resfriado y el **dolor de cabeza** que le estaban comenzando. Al tomar el primer bocado sintió que un **diente** se le quebraba. Parece que él no había pelado bien el ajo.

30 Verde fue mi nacimiento, colorado mi vivir. Y negro me voy poniendo cuando me voy a morir.

El café.

My birth is green,
my life is red.
And I become black
as I reach my end.
(The coffee bean.)

En el mundo hispánico se toma mucho **café**. Por lo tanto muchos países se dedican al cultivo de este preciado grano. En algunos casos la producción no es sólo para el consumo local, sino también para la exportación masiva.

31 Tiene saco verde, y usa chaleco colorado con botones negros.

La sandía.

It has a green coat
and wears a red vest
adorned with black buttons.
(A watermelon.)

A. Parece que Jorge se vistió deslumbrantemente para la fiesta.
B. No hay duda. Lleva puesto **un saco verde** y **un chaleco colorado** con **botones negros**. Parece que va a una fiesta de frutas.
A. ¿Por qué dices eso?
B. Porque parece **una sandía**.

Section Four

Los objetos

Things

32 ¿Qué es lo que se compra para comer y no se come?

La cuchara.

What is purchased to eat and is not eaten?
(A spoon.)

A. Alfredito, no te metas tanto **la cuchara** en la boca.
B. ¿Por qué, mami?
A. Porque **la cuchara** se usa para comer, pero no se come.

33 ¿Qué cosa pequeña se pone en una esquina y le da la vuelta al mundo?

El sello.

What small item is put into a corner and goes around the world?
(A stamp.)

A. Es interesante que este **sello** tan pequeño en esa esquinita va a llevar esta carta a Japón.
B. Sí, y tan barato. Yo no la llevaría ni por cien dólares.
A. Peor. Tú no irías al colmadito de la esquina por lo que cuesta **el sello**.

34 Cruda no se consigue y cocinada no se come.

La ceniza.

Raw you cannot find it, and cooked you would not eat it.
(Ashes.)

A. Por favor, no dejes que **la ceniza** caiga en la alfombra. La última vez que me visitaste dejaste **ceniza** por todos lados.
B. No te preocupes. Ya dejé de fumar y sólo sujeto el cigarrillo completamente apagado. Así la producción de **ceniza** es mínima.
A. ¡Óyeme, qué ingenioso!

35 Tiene dos agujas y no cose.

El reloj.

It has two needles and does not sew.
(A clock.)

The word "agujas" is used for both needles and the hands of a clock.

Las agujas del reloj marcan las dos de la tarde. Teresa se apresura porque tiene que ir a la tienda a comprar **unas agujas** para terminar de coser la camisa de su esposo.

36 Tengo ruedas y pedales, cadena y un manillar. Te ahorro la gasolina aunque te haga sudar.

La bicicleta.

I have wheels and pedals,
chain and handlebar.
I'll save you gas
but I'll make you perspire.
(A bicycle.)

Alfonso se montó en su **bicicleta** y viajó a su oficina por unas cinco millas. Al llegar notó que estaba empapado en sudor y que las piernas estaban un poco resentidas. Pero solamente el pensamiento de haber ahorrado gasolina lo consoló.

37 Estoy escondida en un rincón, cuando hay basura entro en acción.

La escoba.

I am hidden
in a corner.
When there is dirt
I go into action.
(A broom.)

La escoba se siente triste en su rincón porque hace varios días que no la usan. Aunque ve polvo en el piso de la cocina, se mantiene junto a la pared. Repentinamente una mano la agarra y comienza a barrer el piso. El espíritu de **la escoba** se revive mientras entra en acción. Ahora sí que está alegre otra vez.

38 Es tanto lo que me quiere el hombre en su necio orgullo, que hasta crímenes comete sólo por hacerme suyo.

El dinero.

I am desired with such emotion
that man with his foolish pride
will even commit crimes
to make me his own.
(Money.)

A. A mí me gustaría tener mucho mucho **dinero**.
B. ¿Por qué? Tú sabes que **el dinero** no compra todo en la vida.
A. ¡Claro que sí! Uno puede comprar lo que quiera.
B. No, no tienes razón. El dinero no puede comprar amor, felicidad o lealtad.

39 Soy chiquitito, muy chiquitito, pero pongo fin a todo escrito.

El punto.

I am small, so very small,
yet I put an end to all that is written.
(A period.)

Carmen Ana estaba muy enojada. Se sentó a escribir la nota con determinación y al continuar escribiendo sintió desahogo. Cuando terminó el escrito marcó **un punto** exageradamente grande como para acentuar que el asunto estaba absolutamente terminado. Sin embargo esto era innecesario, pues **el punto**, aunque pequeño, le pone fin a todo escrito.

40 El que lo hace, no lo disfruta. El que lo disfruta, no lo ve. El que lo ve, no lo desea. Adivina lo que es.

El ataúd.

He who makes it does not use it.
He who uses it does not see it.
He who sees it does not want it.
Guess what it is.
(A coffin.)

A. Tengo que terminar este **ataúd** para el jueves.
B. ¿Has pensado alguna vez que tú lo haces, pero no lo disfrutas?
A. Um, lo interesante es que el que lo disfruta no lo ve, y yo que lo veo, no lo quiero para nada.

41 Hecha o deshecha, siempre quieta y tumbada esperando tu llegada.

La cama.

It is made or unmade.
Always still and lying down,
it awaits your arrival.
(A bed.)

Enrique siempre tiene ideas graciosas y raras. Él piensa que no hay ninguna amiga como **la cama**. Él dice que su **cama** siempre está tranquila esperando su llegada.

42 Pequeño como un ratón y cuida la casa como un león.

El candado.

It's small like a mouse
and guards your house
like a lion.
(A padlock.)

A. ¿Puedes creer que los ladrones me han robado de la casa tres veces?
B. ¿Qué vas a hacer? ¿Te vas a comprar un perro o un león?
A. Ninguno de los dos. Me voy a comprar algo más barato y más seguro.
B. ¿Qué?
A. Un buen **candado**.

43 Todos andan por mí; yo no ando con nadie. Todos preguntan por mí y yo no pregunto por nadie.

La calle.

Everyone walks on me;
I don't walk with anyone.
Everyone asks about me
and I don't ask about anyone.
(A street.)

A. ¿Dónde queda **la calle** Madrid?
B. Usted está parado en ella. Hoy todos preguntan por esta **calle**. ¿Hay algún acontecimiento especial?
A. Sí, hay un concierto de música latinoamericana gratis.
B. Bueno, entonces voy para allá también para que nadie me siga preguntando las direcciones.

44 Alto y alto como un pino y pesa menos que un comino.

El humo.

It's tall, as tall as a pine tree,
and weighs less than a cumin seed.
(Smoke.)

Norberto aceptó finalmente que estaba perdido en el bosque. Ya desesperado, decidió prender el fuego. Tal vez alguien podría ver **el humo**, que seguramente sobrepasaría los altos pinos, y vendría a rescatarlo.

45 Suelo ir de mano en mano. Sin ser árbol tengo hojas. Como cofre guardo tesoros. ¿Quién soy yo?

El libro.

I tend to go from person to person;
I'm not a tree but I have leaves;
I store treasures like a chest.
What am I?
(A book.)

"Hojas" is a word used for leaves of a plant or tree but is also utilized for pages of a book or notebook.

Es otoño, hace un poco de frío y **las hojas** de los árboles caen en montones. Mientras adentro en la casa, Aurelio escribe arduamente en **las hojas de papel** tratando de describir la belleza del momento.

46 Blanca como la leche
y negra como la pez;
habla sin tener lengua
y camina sin tener pies.

La carta.

It's white as milk
and black as tar.
It talks and has no tongue;
it walks and has no feet.
(A letter.)

Ramón escribía su nota con tinta negra en el blanco papel. El sabía que su **carta** llegaría a su destino e informaría lo sucedido con un toque más personal que un mero mensaje electrónico.

Section Five

No hay que buscar tanto

Don't Look Too Far

47 ¿Por qué el perro mueve la cola?

Porque la cola no mueve al perro.

Why does the dog wag its tail?
(Because the tail cannot wag the dog.)

48 ¿Cómo se pasa un puente que se está cayendo?

Con miedo.

How do you cross a bridge that is falling down? *(With fear.)*

49 ¿Cómo puede volar un avión debajo del agua?

Que esté lloviendo.

How is it possible for an airplane to fly under water?
(If it is raining.)

50 ¿Dónde se para el policía para tocar el pito?

Detrás del pito.

Where does the policeman stand to blow his whistle?
(Behind the whistle.)

51 ¿Por qué la palma tira la hoja al piso?

Porque no se puede doblar a ponerla.

Why does the palm tree drop its leaves to the ground? *(Because it cannot bend down to put them there.)*

52 ¿Cómo llaman en Alemania a los bomberos?

Por teléfono.

How do they call the firemen in Germany? *(By phone.)*

53 ¿Qué es lo que yo necesito para prender un cigarrillo?

Que esté apagado.

What is needed to light a cigarette?
(It needs to be unlit.)

54 ¿Qué es lo que más pone la gallina?

Las patas en el piso.

What is it that the hen "pone" most?
(Its feet on the ground.)

This is a difficult translation since there is a play on the verb "poner." The hen lays eggs, which in Spanish is "poner huevos," but also puts its feet on the ground, "poner las patas en el piso."

A. Yo quiero comprar unas gallinas que **pongan** muchos huevos para venderlos y ganarme un dinerito.

B. Las mías producen muchos huevos pero a veces entran a la casa y la ensucian.

A. Yo no voy a permitir que las mías **pongan** sus patas en el piso de la casa. ¡No!

Section Six

¿Qué le dijo ____ a ____?

What Did ____ Say to ____?

55 ¿Qué le dijo la montaña a la mujer?

«Yo también tengo falda.»

What did the mountain say to the woman?
("I also have a skirt.")

"Falda" is a skirt but also the slope of a mountain.

A. Carmen, quítate **la falda** y ponte unos mahones. Va a ser más fácil y cómodo para ti.
B. No, yo puedo subir la montaña así.
A. Te apuesto que sólo vamos a llegar a **la falda de la montaña** y ya te darás cuenta que yo tenía razón.

56 ¿Qué le dijo la leche al azúcar?

«Nos vemos en el café.»

What did the milk say to the sugar?
("See you in the café.")

"Café" here is used as the tasty stimulant drink as well as the place where you can go to drink it.

A los Pérez siempre les gustaba tomarse su tacita de **café** en **el café** de la esquina de la Avenida Morazán. Ellos pensaban que **el café** del Restaurante Alpino no era tan sabroso.

57 ¿Qué le dijo un jaguar a otro jaguar?

«Jaguaryu?»

What did one jaguar say to another jaguar?
("How are you?")

This riddle plays with the way the greeting "How are you?" sounds to Spanish speakers.

58 ¿Qué le dijo un árbol a otro?

«Nos dejaron plantados.»

What did one tree say to another?
("They stood us up.")

"Plantar" means to plant; "dejar plantado" refers to failing to keep an appointment with someone, or in other words, standing someone up.

A. La actividad comenzaba a las ocho e íbamos a **plantar** un árbol en honor a los dos maestros.
B. ¿Qué pasó? ¿Por qué no llevaron a cabo la actividad?
A. Marcos nunca llegó. Nos **dejó plantados**.

59 ¿Qué le dijo la oreja al dedo?

«No pase porque está encerado.»

What did the ear say to the finger?
("Don't come in because it is waxed.")

60 ¿Qué le dijo el fósforo al cigarrillo?

«Por ti perdí la cabeza.»

What did the match say to the cigarette?
("Because of you I lost my head.")

The ignitable end of the matchstick is called "la cabeza" in Spanish. "Perder la cabeza" means to go crazy.

Pedro estaba desesperado porque su esposa lo había abandonado. Verdaderamente él **había perdido la cabeza** y fumaba incontrolablemente. Tanta era su locura que cada vez que prendía un cigarrillo tomaba el fósforo en sus manos y le decía "tú también **perdiste la cabeza**."

61 ¿Qué le dijo un cable a otro?

«Somos los intocables.»

What did one cable say to another?
("We are the untouchables.")

Usually cables have a high charge of electricity and no one wants to touch them. Also, the TV series "The Untouchables" was well-known in Latin America and was translated as "Los intocables."

62 ¿Qué le dijo la cuchara a la gelatina?

«¡No tiembles, cobarde!»

What did the spoon say to the Jell-O?
("Don't shake, you coward!")

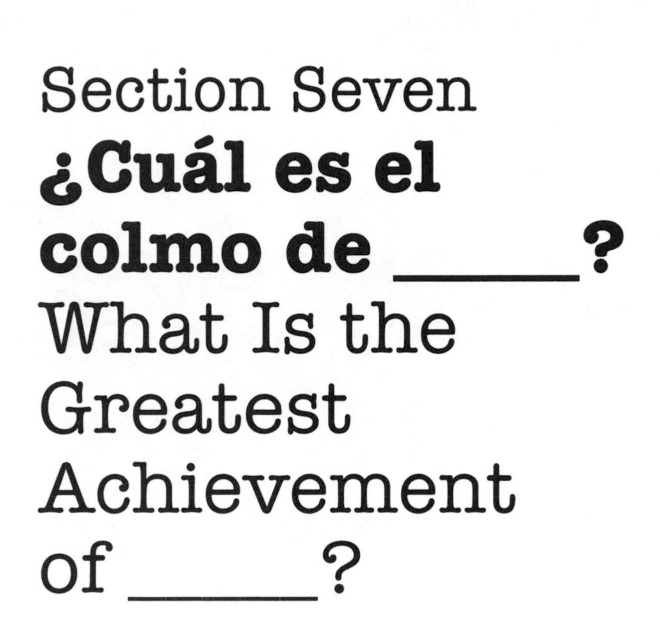

Section Seven
¿Cuál es el colmo de _____?
What Is the Greatest Achievement of _____?

63 ¿Cuál es el colmo de un oso panda?

Sacarse una foto a color y salir a blanco y negro.

What is the greatest achievement of a panda bear? *(To have a color photo taken and come out in black and white.)*

64 ¿Cuál es el colmo de un jardinero?

Que su mujer lo deje plantado.

What is the greatest achievement of a gardener? *(To have his wife stand him up.)*

Here there is a play on words with the verb "plantar," which means to plant, and "dejar plantado" which refers to being stood up.

65 ¿Cuál es el colmo de un soldado?

Tener un hijo soldador.

What is the greatest achievement of a soldier?
(To have a son who is a welder.)

The playfulness of this question and answer lies in the similarities of sound between "soldado" and "soldador," which are two completely different vocations. "Un soldado" is a soldier and "un soldador" is a welder.

66 ¿Cuál es el colmo de un dentista?

Hacerle una caja de dientes a la boca del estómago.

What is the greatest achievement of a dentist?
(To make dentures for the "mouth" of the stomach.)

The esophageal opening of the stomach is called "la boca del estómago" in Spanish.

El abuelo y el nieto jugaban a la lucha libre cuando el abuelo recibió un golpe en **la boca del estómago**. El golpe fue tan fuerte que éste tuvo que abrir **la boca** y **la caja de dientes** salió disparada. El abuelo cogió su **caja de dientes** como si nada hubiera pasado y se la metió a **la boca**. Ambos rieron descontroladamente.

67 ¿Cuál es el colmo de un peluquero?

Hacerle un permanente a la cabeza del ajo.

What is the greatest achievement of a hairdresser? *(To give a permanent to a "head" of garlic.)*

The whole garlic bulb is called "una cabeza de ajo" in Spanish.

A. Aurora, quiero que me peines y me pongas guapa.
B. ¿Qué quieres que te haga?
A. Quiero que me hagas **un permanente**.
B. Teresa, por Dios. ¡Tu pelo es tan corto y tan finito que sería más fácil hacerle **un permanente a una cabeza de ajo**!

68 ¿Cuál es el colmo de un electricista?

Que la esposa se llame Luz y la hija Lucerito.

What is the greatest achievement of an electrician? *(That his wife's name be Luz and his daughter's name Lucerito.)*

"Luz," meaning light, and "Lucerito," a little bright star, are both common Spanish names.

69 ¿Cuál es el colmo de una enfermera?

Poner una inyección en la vena Quaker.

What is the greatest achievement of a nurse?
(To give an injection in the "Quaker vein.")

The words "la avena," meaning oats, when pronounced together sound like "la vena" or vein. Quaker Oats, then, becomes a pivotal piece to understanding this word puzzle.

Section Eight

La contestación está en la adivinanza

The Answer Is in the Riddle

70 Oro no es,
plata no es.
Quítale el ropón
y verás lo que es.

El plátano.

It is not gold;
it is not silver.
Remove its garments
and you'll see what it is.
(A plantain.)

The second line gives the answer to this well-known riddle by saying that "plátano es" or "plantain it is."

71 Te la digo y te la digo
y te la vuelvo a decir,
y si no la adivinas,
te la vuelvo a repetir.

La tela.

I tell it to you and I tell it to you
and I tell it to you again.
And if you cannot guess it,
I'll repeat it to you again.
(A cloth or fabric.)

Here the object pronouns "te" (you) and "la" (it) come together to form the answer, "tela."

72 Largo largo como un tren, y lo es, y lo es.

El hilo.

It is long, long like a train,
and that it is, and that it is.
(A thread.)

By using the imagination and making some minor perception changes, the participant can find the answer in the last line, where "y lo es, y lo es" (and that it is, and that it is) becomes "hilo es, hilo es" (thread it is, thread it is).

73 Te digo y te repito que si no adivinas, no vales un pito.

El té.

I will tell you once and I will tell you twice.
And if you cannot guess it,
you're not worth a hill of beans.
(Tea.)

The answer to this riddle appears in the first line when the noun "té" (tea) is inserted and replaces the object pronoun "te" (you).

74 Soy blanda, dulce y amarilla
y a todo el mundo agrado.
Si quieres saber mi nombre,
espera, ¿estás enterado?

La pera.

I am soft, sweet and yellow
and pleasing to everyone.
If you want to know my name,
just wait, did you catch on?
(A pear.)

"Espera" (wait) is the key term and answer when it is pronounced as two words, "es pera" (it is pear).

75 Un gordito rojito que no toma café, sólo toma té. Adivina qué es.

El tomate.

It's chubby and red
and doesn't drink coffee;
it only drinks tea.
Guess what it is.
(A tomato.)

In the third line, "sólo toma té" means "only drinks tea," yet with only a slight change in inflection, the phrase can sound like "sólo tomate" (only tomato).

76 Siempre va llena
y nunca vacía;
la ve grandota
el que la mira.

La ballena.

It always is full
and never is empty;
it appears large
to the one who sees it.
(A whale.)

"Va llena" means "it goes full," but when said together the phrase sounds like only one word, "ballena" (whale). This linguistic playfulness is possible since the letters "b" and "v" are both pronounced as "b" in Spanish.

77 El enamorado,
si eres advertido,
te dije mi nombre
y el de mi vestido.

Elena Mora. Morado.

Lover,
if you are sharp,
I told you my name
and the color of my dress.
(Elena Mora. Purple.)

By making the necessary adaptations in inflection, the first line provides the two answers to the riddle questions. It is interesting to note that a translation of the speaker's name would be "Helen Blackberry."

Section Nine

Hay que pensar un poquito más

Think a Little Bit Harder

78 ¿Qué es lo que no se ve ni se puede coger?

El viento.

What can neither be seen nor be grasped?
(The wind.)

79 ¿Qué es lo que mientras más seca más moja?

La toalla.

What is it that the more it dries the wetter it becomes?
(A towel.)

A. Jacobo, por favor, seca el piso del baño después que te duches.
B. ¿Por qué?
A. Porque me mojo los pies, y es resbaloso y me puedo caer.
B. Está bien, mami, pero hay un problemita. Es que si uso **una toalla se seca** el piso, pero **se moja la toalla**.
A. ¡Ay, mi hijo, qué dilema!

80 ¿Qué es lo que se rompe de tan sólo nombrarlo?

El silencio.

What breaks by merely mentioning its name? *(Silence.)*

81 ¿Qué es lo que entra antes que uno a un sitio cerrado?

La llave.

What enters before you do into a locked place?
(A key.)

82 ¿Qué cosa será y es de entender que cuanto más le quita más grande es?

El hoyo.

What can it be and is understood to be that the more one takes from it, the larger it becomes?
(A hole.)

83 ¿En qué se parece una torre a una bomba?

En que la torre está allá y la bomba estalla.

In what way is a tower like a bomb?
(In that the tower is "over there" and the bomb "explodes.")

"Está allá" (is over there) and "estalla" (explodes) sound the same orally in Spanish.

A. La bomba que prepararon para destruir el edificio no **estalla**. ¿Qué pasará?

B. No sé. Vamos a preguntarle a Federico que es el experto. ¿Dónde está él?

A. Él **está allá**, cerca de la torre de control.

84 ¿Qué Dios le da al hombre dos veces, gratis, y si la pierde por tercera vez tiene que comprarla?

La dentadura.

What does God give us twice free of charge, but if it's lost the third time, it needs to be purchased?
(A set of teeth.)

A. Tengo una cita con el dentista a las dos de la tarde.
B. ¿Vas a que te empasten una muela?
A. No, voy a que el dentista me proporcione **la dentadura**. Si prestas atención te darás cuenta que el Gran Creador me proporcionó gratis las otras dos **dentaduras**. Esta vez, desafortunadamente voy a tener que pagar un ojo de la cara.

85 ¿Por qué el cerdo anda con la cabeza baja, mirando al piso?

Porque se siente avergonzado de que su madre sea una cerda.

Why does the pig walk around with his head down, looking at the ground?
(Because it is ashamed that its mother is a pig.)

86 ¿Qué cosa es que mientras más grande es menos se ve?

La obscuridad.

What is it
that the bigger it is
the less it can be seen?
(Darkness.)

87 Un tío tiene una hermana que no es tía mía. ¿Qué queda de mí?

Es mi madre.

An uncle has a sister
who is not my aunt.
What is she to me?
(She is my mother.)

88 Si la tienes, la buscas, y si no la tienes ni la buscas ni la quieres.

La pulga.

If you have it, you look for it,
and if you don't have it,
you neither look for it nor desire it.
(A flea.)

89 Un árbol con doce ramas, en cada una cuatro nidos, en cada uno siete huevos siempre viejos, siempre nuevos.

El año.

A tree with twelve branches:
on each branch four nests,
in each nest seven eggs.
Always old; always new.
(A year.)

In this poetic word puzzle, the twelve branches refer to the months of the year, the four nests symbolize the weeks, and the seven eggs the days.

90 **¿Qué es más grande que Dios**
y peor que el diablo?
El pobre lo tiene,
el rico lo necesita,
y si lo comes, te morirás.

Nada.

What is greater than God
and more evil than the devil?
The poor have it,
the rich need it,
and if you eat it, you will die.
(Nothing.)

91 ¿Con cúales tres números iguales, que no sean 4, se hace 12?

1 + **11**

What three numbers that are equal, without using 4, will make a sum of 12?
(1 + 11)

92 Dime dos monedas que suman treinta centavos, y una no es de veinticinco.

Una no es de veinticinco centavos porque es de cinco, pero la otra sí es una moneda de veinticinco centavos.

Tell me which two coins add up to thirty, and one is not a quarter.
(One coin is not a quarter because it is a nickel, but the other one is indeed a quarter.)

93 **Un señor tiene que cruzar un lago en una lancha. Tiene que pasar en ella, uno a la vez, un león, una cabra y una yerba. ¿Cómo puede hacer él para que el león no se coma la cabra y para que la cabra no se coma la yerba?**

Primero pasa la cabra al otro lado. Regresa y se lleva el león y se trae la cabra y la deja. Se lleva la yerba y la deja con el león. Entonces, regresa y busca la cabra.

A man traveling with a goat, a lion, and a quantity of grass needs to cross a lake in a small boat. If he can take with him only one of these at a time, how can he do so without the lion eating the goat or the goat eating the grass?
(The man first takes the goat to the other side. He returns, takes the lion across, brings the goat back and leaves it on the original side. Next he takes the grass across and leaves it with the lion. Then he returns again and transports the goat.)

Section Ten

Un juego de palabras

A Play on Words

94 ¿Por qué el perro le ladra al automóvil?

Porque el automóvil lleva un gato en el baúl.

Why does the dog bark at a car?
(Because the car has a "gato" in the trunk.)

"Gato" is the word for a cat but also means a car jack. In some places, the term "gata," or female cat, is used for the tool.

Alfonso iba por la carretera a toda velocidad mientras **su gato** Misuri dormía plácidamente en el asiento trasero. De repente el carro cogió un hueco y una llanta comenzó a desinflarse. Alfonso sacó **el gato** del baúl y comenzó a cambiar la llanta. Misuri, mientras tanto, observaba la acción desde el cristal trasero.

95 ¿En qué se parece un preso a un marido?

Ambos tienen esposas.

In what way are a prisoner and a husband alike?
(Both have "esposas.")

"Esposas" is used in Spanish to designate both "wives" and "handcuffs."

La policía, finalmente, pudo alcanzar y detener el carro de Humberto. Inmediatamente lo sacaron del carro y le pusieron **las esposas**. Mientras se lo llevaban al carro patrulla, **su esposa** observaba el incidente preguntándose lo que iba a pasar con él.

96 ¿En qué se parece una iglesia cerrada a un tuberculoso?

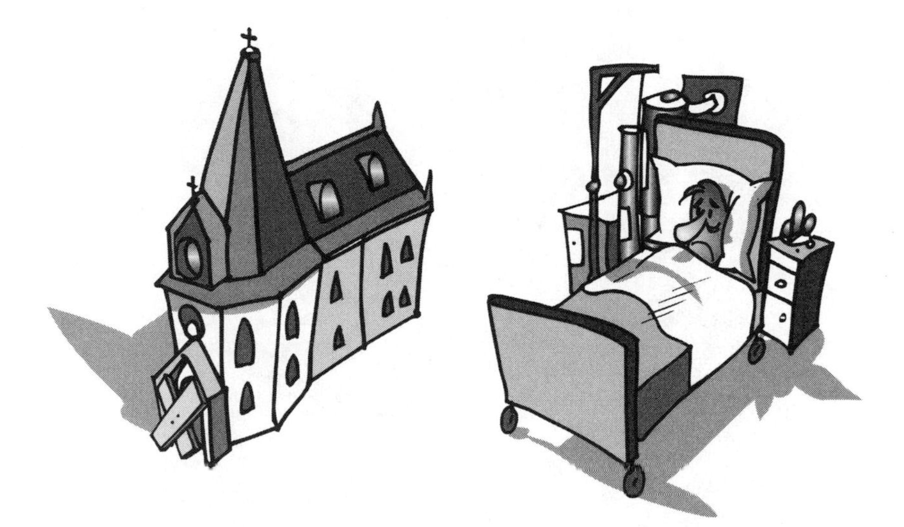

Ninguno tiene cura.

In what way is a closed church like a person with tuberculosis?
(Neither has a "cura.")

The words "el cura" are used for priest and "la cura" for a cure.

A. Yo estoy muy orgullosa de mi hijo. El quiere ser **cura** en la Iglesia Santa Teresita.

B. El mío desea ser médico y encontrar **la cura** del cáncer.

A. Ambas debemos estar muy orgullosas, pues ambos oficios son muy nobles.

97 ¿Cuántas cabezas tiene una gallina?

Una cabeza y pico.

How many heads does a hen have?
(One head and "pico.")

"Pico" is used in Spanish to indicate "a little bit more"; it also means "beak."

A. ¿Cuántas gallinas compraste?
B. Compré ciento y **pico**.
A. ¿Tú crees que se van a herir unas a otras en el gallinero?
B. Yo pienso cortarles **el pico** para que no suceda eso.

98 Yo tengo calor y frío y no frío sin calor.

La sartén.

I am hot and cold
and "no frío" without heat.
(A frying pan.)

It is impossible to translate this riddle without giving the answer away. The wordplay rests upon "frío," which means "cold" as an adjective or noun and "to fry" when used as a verb in first person singular.

A. Por favor, prende el aire acondicionado porque si no me **frío** del calor que hace.
B. Este aire no funciona bien y enfría demasiado.
A. No hay problema. A mí me gusta más **el frío** que el calor.

99 Entre más cerca más largo y entre más largo más cerca.

La cerca.

The more "cerca," the longer it is,
and the longer it is, the more "cerca."
(A fence.)

This is one of the most difficult Spanish riddles to translate literally without giving away the answer. "Cerca" means close, as in measuring distance, but is also the Spanish term for a fence of whatever construction material.

Verdaderamente la casa de Bernardo quedaba **cerca** de la de Carmelo, a sólo cien metros. Sin embargo había **una cerca** de alambre que impedía tomar la ruta más corta a las casas.

100 Soy un hombre con cabeza, sin manos y con un pie. Dieron sobre mi cabeza y al mismo Jesús sujeté.

El clavo.

I am a man with a head,
without hands and with one foot.
They hit me on my head
and Jesus himself I held up.
(A nail.)

A. No, absolutamente no quiero meterme en ese asunto.

B. ¿Por qué? Él es tu hermano, tu familia.

A. No deseo inmiscuirme en problemas ajenos. Uno siempre sale de malas.

B. Bueno, parece que tú tendrás que ser tratado como **el clavo**: hay que darte por la cabeza para que recapacites y te metas. Espero no recurrir a este método. ¿Por qué no piensas en cómo ayudar?

101 Cogí un pato con una pata y lo eché dentro de un barril. ¿Cuántos patos y patas había en el barril?

Un pato cojo.

I caught and put a duck with a "pata"
into a barrel.
How many ducks
are in the barrel?
(One limping duck.)

The translation here is difficult to make without giving away the answer. "Pata" is a female duck, but it is also the leg of an animal.

Jorge y Enrique compraron cinco patos y tres **patas**. Entre ellos había uno que tenía **una pata** un poco incapacitada, sin embargo éste compartía con los demás sin mayores limitaciones.

Translations

NOTE: Numbers refer to riddle numbers, and not to page numbers.

1.

A. **The sun** is very large and is always **on fire**. Although it is far away from us, it can **burn us** if we get too much sun. Also, its ultraviolet rays can be harmful.
B. Maybe a few **candles** would not be so dangerous.
A. But imagine how many **candles** we would need!
B. Many, many—certainly a lot of them!

2.

A. What big **ears** Manolín has!
B. Yes, you're right. At least he takes them with him every place he goes. The problem is he cannot see them.
A. Of course, only when he looks in the mirror.

3.

A. Those mango trees are not producing well at all.
B. At least **the hens** can sleep there during the night.
A. Ha-ha! The value of those trees goes up at night.

4.

The Marrero brothers are very **united**. They live in the same house, share all their things, and always travel together. The people of the town say that they are like **the fingers** of your hand that always are together.

5.

A. People say **the eyes** are the mirror of your soul.
B. I think they are right.
A. Of course. They are like **two transparent orbs** through which you can see into the human soul.
B. Hey, Juan, you are getting poetic.

6.

A. That **bull** always likes to go to the field **at night**.
B. Yes, and it seems as though the reflection of the moon in the water makes him run with great enthusiasm.
A. You know, one night I saw that impressive animal run so fast that not even the fiercest **dog** would have been able to stop it. It seemed that **the bull** and **the night** became one.

7.

A. Marcela, you talk about everybody! It seems like your **tongue** is always on the move.
B. Of course, that old lady has to be taken out of her prison once in a while, don't you think?
A. In your case, probably so. You'd probably say that you want to let her get dry, too. What a pair of women you two are!

8.

A. I really prefer **cotton** fabric.
B. Why? There are other very good materials.
A. For me, cloth that is made out of **cotton** is fresh, lasts a long time, and comes through a natural process.
B. Sounds pretty good. Are you sure this isn't a paid advertisement?

9.

A. I've been reading that there are four elements essential for the survival of the human being: water, earth, fire, and **air**.
B. Well, in my thinking the most important and interesting one of the group is **air**.
A. Why **air**?
B. Because even though we don't see it, it is always with us. In addition, we cannot live without it. In other words, **air** and I are inseparable.

10.

A. It's raining and yet the sun is shining. Hey, look at that incredible **rainbow**.
B. Hurry, get the camera and let's take a picture of it.
A. Even better, let's paint it so we can highlight its colors one by one.
B. Good idea, that way we can create a masterpiece like one of Picasso's.
A. I don't think so!

11.

The two men entered the abandoned house in search of things of value. The darkness of the night made it impossible for them to see much farther than their faces. Suddenly both of them saw something that seemed to stretch and shrink as they moved. They froze in their steps, holding their breath. Then simultaneously they relaxed, almost laughing—it was only their **shadow**.

12.

The little old lady on the park bench had captured the interest of some children nearby with her riddles. As she told of the two, and the five, and the thirty-two that had eaten a mango, her listeners guessed she was talking about an army. "Oh, no," she chuckled, "it is **the eyes**, **the fingers**, and **the teeth** of only one person!"

13.

A. What is the capital of Argentina?
B. I don't know. Santiago?
A. Buenos Aires, Felicia, what do you have in your head?
B. In my head? Nothing, my friend. On my head? **Lice**. Plenty of **lice**.

14.

The man turned off the light and crawled into bed with his wife. About two minutes later they were startled by a strange whooshing noise above them. Somewhat shaken, the man climbed out of bed and turned on the light. To their surprise, they saw a **bat** now clinging onto a curtain. After a few minutes of chasing it around the room, the little animal left through the same open window it had entered.

15.

The cowboy took his **horse** to the blacksmith because **a horseshoe** was loose. The careful craftsman tied the animal by the **head** and proceeded to examine its foot. He discovered that **the heads** of several **nails** had come out.

16.

In a thoughtless experiment, the young lad wound the rope of **a goat** around his own neck. He wanted to prove to himself that he was stronger than the animal. Startled by the tug on the rope, **the goat** took off running recklessly and dragged the young experimenter all over the farm. As the rope gradually unwound, the boy was left with a neck covered with blood. A lesson was learned from that incident: **A goat** is stronger than a boy.

17.

A. What are your hobbies?
B. I don't have any hobbies.
A. I collect **escarabajos** (**beetles**).
B. You know, if hobbies can help to eliminate stress, maybe I should start collecting something.
A. Why don't you try collecting "es cara arribas"?
B. You and your twisted imagination!

18.

A. I drink chamomile tea when I cannot sleep.
B. I drink a cup of hot milk.
A. Some people count **sheep**.
B. I don't think that works. That's only a myth.

19.

A. I am terrified of **snakes**.
B. Why? There are **snakes** that are harmless and won't do anything to you. Others don't harm you unless you provoke them. **Snakes** are important in nature's cycle, you know. Also, some have gorgeous colors.
A. I don't know. It's just the idea for me that they can be anywhere and might bite you.

20.

A. When I was in second grade our teacher taught us a song about **a chick**.
B. What a coincidence! Mine also did that in second grade.
A. The song talked about **a chick** that was hungry and was cold, and said "peep, peep." It was one of our most-sung songs.
B. It looks like **chicks** are favorite pets of children.

21.

Federico's **cat** is big and black. Truly it is a pretty **cat**, but I personally think it is very spoiled. You see, the beloved animal goes out only at night, drinks only fresh milk, and demands only the best meat to eat.

____

22.

The eagle is an impressive bird. When flying, it looks like it rules the whole field. There are countries that use this bird as a symbol in their coat of arms or monetary system. Also, there are many sports teams that have **the eagle** as their mascot.

____

23.

A. Margarita, peel **the onions**, please.
B. No, Mommy, you peel them. These horrible things always make me cry.
A. My daughter, if you do not peel them right now, I'll be the one making you cry.

____

24.

A. Paco, please pass me the **salt**.
B. Man, you shouldn't keep using so much **salt**. It's not good for your health.
A. It may not be good for my health, but it surely feels good to my taste buds.

____

25.

A. These days people eat a lot of meat and not enough vegetables.
B. Yes I know, stuff like hamburgers, hot dogs, and pork chops.
A. In my opinion, what can be better than a good salad? You can throw together tomatoes, lettuce, broccoli, and **cauliflower**. Then you put on several sprinkles of good olive oil, and with a thick slice of homemade bread you have a satisfying and healthy meal.

____

26.

Wheat flour is used in a multitude of products. Tasty bread in a variety of forms, delicious cookies, and a great diversity of pastries are only some of the ways in which **wheat** is used.

____

27.

Stealthily the man climbed the fence and crawled up into the tree in search of some golden sweet **oranges**. He had picked only the first one, when to his dismay he heard the angry shout of a man intent on protecting his fruit. The **orange**-hunter did not wait to see the owner's face.

28.

A. You can go ahead and peel **the pineapple** for the fruit salad for supper.
B. OK, but do you know what I think I will do? I am going to keep **the crown** and plant it in my garden tomorrow.
A. That's a good idea, but while you are peeling the fruit, be sure to take out all **the eyes**.
B. Whatever you say. The only problem is that if I take out its **eyes** it won't be able to see.
A. You are so funny! You and your weak jokes!

29.

Pedro grabbed **the whole garlic bulb** and took out **a clove**. Then he sliced it and made a sandwich to cure a cold and **headache** that were just beginning. Upon taking the first bite he felt his **tooth** had chipped. Apparently he had not thoroughly peeled the garlic.

30.

In the Hispanic world **coffee** is consumed a lot. For this reason, many countries devote a great deal of their economy to the cultivation of the valued bean. In many cases the production is not only for local consumption, but also for major exportation.

31.

A. Looks like Jorge dressed himself in a dazzling way for the party.
B. That's for sure. He left wearing **a green coat** and **a red vest** with **black buttons**. It looks like he's going to a fruit party.
A. Why do you say that?
B. Because he looks like **a watermelon**!

32.

A. Alfredito, please do not stick your **spoon** so deep into your mouth.
B. Why, Mommy?
A. Because **the spoon** is used for eating and is not to be eaten.

33.

A. It is interesting that **a stamp** as small as this one in a corner of an envelope will take this letter all the way to Japan.
B. Yes, and so cheaply. I would not take it that far for a hundred dollars.
A. Worse yet. You would not even go to the corner store for the cost of **the stamp**!

34.

A. Please do not let the **ashes** fall on the carpet. The last time you visited me you left **ashes** everywhere.
B. Don't worry. I stopped smoking and I only hold the unlit cigarette for effect. That way there aren't any **ashes**.
A. Hey, that's smart.

35.

The clock's hands are showing two o'clock in the afternoon. Teresa hurries up because she has to go to the store to buy **needles** to finish sewing a shirt for her husband.

36.

Alfonso jumped on his **bicycle** and traveled to his office five miles away. Upon arriving, he noticed he was soaked with sweat and that his legs were feeling a bit sore. Yet for him the overriding consolation was the gas he was able to save.

37.

The broom feels sad in its corner because it has not been used for several days. Even though it can see dust on the kitchen floor, it remains propped against the wall. Suddenly a hand grabs it and starts to sweep the floor. **The broom**'s spirit soars as it is put into action. Now indeed it feels happy again.

38.

A. I would love to have oodles and oodles of **money**.
B. Why so? You know **money** does not buy everything in life.
A. Of course it does! One can buy whatever you want.
B. Nope, you're wrong. **Money** cannot buy love, happiness, or loyalty.

39.

Carmen Ana was very angry. She sat down and wrote the note with determination, and as she continued writing, she felt increasing relief. After the final sentence, she formed an exaggeratedly big **period** as though to emphasize that the matter was absolutely finished. In reality this final action was unnecessary since **the period**, no matter how small, puts an end to all that is written.

40.

A. I have to finish this **coffin** for Thursday.
B. Did you ever think about it that you make it, but you don't use it?
A. Hmm, it is interesting that the one who uses it does not see it, and I, seeing it, do not want to use it at all.

41.

Enrique always has funny and unusual ideas. He thinks that there is no better friend than his **bed**. He says his **bed** is always there for him and awaiting his arrival.

42.

A. Would you believe that thieves have robbed my house three times?
B. What are you going to do? Are you going to buy yourself a dog or a lion?
A. Neither. I am going to buy something cheaper and more secure.
B. What?
A. A good **padlock**.

43.

A. Where is Madrid **Street**?
B. You are on it. Everybody is asking for this **street** today. Is there some special event?
A. Yes, there is a free Latin American music concert.
B. Well, then I am going there too so that no one else asks me the way.

44.

Norberto finally accepted that he was lost in the forest. Now desperate, he decided to build a fire. Perhaps somebody would be able to see **the**

smoke that undoubtedly would rise above the tall pine trees and would hopefully come to his rescue.

45.

It is fall, a bit cold, and **the leaves** of the trees are falling in quantities. Meanwhile, inside the house, Aurelio is writing enthusiastically on **sheets of paper** trying to describe the beauty of the moment.

46.

Ramón penned his note by hand using black ink on white paper. He knew his **letter** would arrive at its destination in a timely fashion and would give the information a more personal touch than a mere electronic message.

54.

A. I want to buy some hens that **lay** a lot of eggs so I can sell them and earn some money.
B. Mine produce a lot of eggs but sometimes they get into the house and make a mess.
A. I am not going to permit mine to even **put** their feet onto the floor of my house. No way!

55.

A. Carmen, take off your **skirt** and put on jeans. It will be easier and more comfortable for you.
B. No, I can climb the mountain this way.
A. I bet you that when we reach the **slope of the mountain**, you will see that I was right.

56.

The Pérezes always liked to drink their cup of **coffee** at **the café** on the corner of Morazán Avenue. They thought **the coffee** at the Alpino Restaurant was not as tasty.

58.

A. The activity was beginning at eight o'clock and we were thinking of **planting** a tree in honor of the two teachers.

B. What happened? Why didn't you do it?
A. Marcos never arrived. He **stood us up**.

60.

Pedro was in despair because his wife had left him. He was really **going crazy** and was smoking uncontrollably. His irrationality was such that every time he lit a cigarette, he took the match and told it, "You also **lost your head**!"

66.

Grandfather and grandson were wrestling when the grandpa received a blow to **the upper part of his stomach**. The blow was so hard that he had to open **his mouth**, and **his dentures** shot out like a bullet. Grandpa picked up **his dentures** as if nothing had even happened, and put them back in **his mouth**. Both grandfather and grandson laughed uncontrollably.

67.

A. Aurora, I want you to do my hair and make me look pretty.
B. What do you want me to do for you?
A. I want you to give me **a permanent**.
B. Good grief, Teresa. Your hair is so short and so fine it would be easier to give **a permanent to a head of garlic**!

79.

A. Jacobo, please, dry the bathroom floor after your shower.
B. Why?
A. Because I get my feet wet and it is slippery and I could fall down.
B. OK, Mom, but there is a little problem. If I use **a towel** the floor gets dry but **the towel gets wet**.
A. Oh my son, what a problem!

83.

A. The bomb that they made to destroy the building is not **exploding**. I wonder what is happening?
B. I do not know. Let's ask Federico, who is the expert. Where is he?
A. He is **over there** close to the control tower.

84.

A. I have a dentist appointment at two o'clock in the afternoon.
B. Are you going to have a tooth filled?
A. No, I am going so my dentist can make me **a set of teeth**. If you think about it you'll see that the Great Creator provided me my other two **sets of teeth** free of charge. This time, unfortunately, I am going to have to pay an arm and a leg.

94.

Alfonso was speeding down the road while **his cat** Misuri was sleeping placidly in the rear seat. Suddenly the car hit a pothole and a tire began to go flat. Alfonso took out **the car jack** from the trunk and began to change the tire. Misuri, meanwhile, observed the action from the rear window.

95.

The police were finally able to catch up and stop Humberto's car. They took him out of the car immediately and **handcuffed** him. While they were taking him to the patrol car, **his wife** was observing the action, wondering what was going to happen to him.

96.

A. I am very proud of my son. He wants to be **a priest** in the Santa Teresita church.
B. Mine wants to be a physician and discover **the cure** for cancer.
A. We both should be very proud; both professions are very noble.

97.

A. How many hens did you buy?
B. I bought a hundred and **some**.
A. Do you think they are going to hurt each other in the henhouse?
B. I am planning to trim their **beaks** so that does not happen.

98.

A. Please turn on the air-conditioning. If not, I'm going **to be fried** with this hot weather!
B. This air conditioning is not working right and is cooling too much.
A. No problem, I like **cold weather** better than hot weather.

99.

In reality Bernardo's house was **close** to Carmelo's house, only one hundred meters away. There was a wire **fence**, though, that kept one from using the shortest route between their houses.

100.

A. No, I absolutely do not want to get involved in this matter.
B. Why not? He is your brother, your family.
A. I don't want to get involved in other people's problems. You always come out in the worst end of the deal.
B. Well, looks like you might need to be treated like **a nail**: you know, get hit on the head so you reconsider and then make an impact. I would hope I would not have to resort to this method with you. Why don't you think how you can help out?

101.

Jorge and Enrique bought five male ducks and three **female ducks**. Among them there was one whose **leg** was somewhat injured. Nevertheless, the duck interacted with the others without major limitation.

Index

NOTE: Numbers refer to riddle numbers, and not to page numbers.